refined [rɪˈtaɪnd]

adj. redefined in the context of a relationship

For H, J, E and now M L

66 *Language, like the people who use it, finds meaning in relationship.*

— James Monhilston

H. Jack Livingstone
worked as a travel writer
for eight years, publishing
in broadsheets and online.

Refined emerged during
his final years abroad in
destinations as diverse as
Italy, Japan and the Middle
East. Each poem refines
a word to create a new
shared meaning between
author and reader.

First published 2017 © Morphē Arts
Cover and Design © Lizzie Kevan Curtis

Contents

Flick

Lake Garda

It was a quick, microbiologically quick, flick,
That click of the eyes locked, sticking;
An instant interest, pure impurity.

Flick.
In the flicker of that flick, two souls
Coursed into each other, surged
Over, until the fear of falling broke
The strangers' flick as quick as a bolt.

Flick.
A demi-second,
Long enough for consciousness to
Snap the shutter, expose a memory
On which to form a fantasy.

Flick – gone.

But the picture holds on,
The fear, the love,
The fear.

And the questions buzz behind upturned lips,
Did she think I flicked at her?
And did she really flick at me?

Refined

In those few fleet weeks
We changed what courage meant
And fear.

When you asked for a brew
I came back flying your cup on a saucer strewn
With a brown lump, or two.

I teased out your catchphrase,
What do you want now?
A memory of your sister
Not meant to mock me.

We refined us in those few weeks
And found finer nuances in each other:
In each other's letters;
And in each other's characters;
And in each other's meanings.

Courage

What do you want now?
She accepts the kisses that nestle in her neck
And speaks all mock-melodramatic-like:
Are you on shore today darling? We should elope!
It would be terribly romantic! The crew would be frantic!
We could lose them in the vineyards!

I tell her I would take her
Anywhere in the world.
If she wants.

Then, with a sigh,
Born of stories unsurfaced,
She stands, her book discarded on the lounger.
The boat rail oranges in the light of Hesperia:

The sea is so unsearchable,
The world so promising,
Sometimes courage is to turn for port.

I'm like cotton knotted on a nail
Caught as she flashes sideways eyes,
When did you last see your family?

Catch

Melted like a crystal glass into splendid sun,
She knew I wasn't a catch to haul aground,
But one to let slip through the grip
And remember in tales that open, 'Once ...'

I was that kind of catch.

She awoke a blue and sunset kingfisher
And I a fish became a river
Looking back
As I coursed away.

Judgment

*Inspired by a boy in Quito with a genetic
condition called Angelman Syndrome*

I was predisposed
To be who I am.

Conceived in the rollicking
Of slack sex
On a shack floor
For thirty dollars;
In other words,
In sin.

My mother said it put splinters in her back
But that's how he wanted it,
He was all animal.
He is all absence.

I have a chromosome missing, they tell me;
Angelman, they call me.
I'm missing data from my mother.

I was pre-disposed
To be who I am.

"Satan was an angel, man," they say.
They are angry because I can not cut my toe nails.
I try but the scissors confuse my fingers.

She says, "That's how it is,
We choose and we don't choose."
But some nights,
We feel sad.
"Is it my fault?" one of us asks
Signing the cross.

Each morning I resolve
Not to stick my index skywards,
Inwards, outwards,
Or growl down a microscope
At sloppy evolution.
"Es así."

Their 'judgment' is my 'struggle'
I will not be disposed.
I am who I am.

Rose

That which we call a rose
By any other name would smell as sweet
— Romeo and Juliet, II.ii

I named my laptop 'Rose'
Her pungence did not differ.

I named a red rose, 'Laptop' –
But still I liked to sniff her.

Snow

Mpopho, Kwazulu-Natal, ZA

Ha! They pour with laughter as I try to click 'ixoxo'
(The x, intending to sound like geeing on a horse,
Comes out closer to choking on a hake!)

Ixoxo
Ixoxo

Snothanda (we call her Snow) wants to be a pilot
Or a netball player when she's a tall woman.
I tell her flight would be an advantage in most sports.
She laughs, though I think she does not understand.

Zulu Snow dreams of the sky,
African Snow, cirrus mist in view,
Squints down, gazing on a hawk.

Her brother, balloon-light, rides my back
Arms over my chest
The others play with stones.

Today Auntie is not at home
The children play alone
Ah! He's clutching on my heart.

Ixoxo
Ixoxo

13

Rehearsal

Jubilee Line, Northbound

Baulk-eyed, vague-gazing shades, grazing gum,
Plastic vapid pacifier, mouth-sticker.
Flowing through the sewage streams of London's
Lethian undercurrent.
Dropping bagel crumbs for secreted metro-rodents
As vacant as vapours, still as a shop front.

"Did you have a nice rehearsal?"

Bobbing through Thanatos' winding tunnels
Stopping frequently to exchange wearied souls.
"There is a good service operating on all lines."
We scour the maps
And learn our lines,
For a time when we too will find ourselves
Underground; Lain or standing. Glazed.

"Good journey?" the boatman asks
As we pay our fees.

We watch as Time slows to a stop.

tune

About to meet the boss, Holborn

shape me now shape me into your design my teacher comply
me to hum no longer the flat off-beat sore attempts at harmony
but the tune the default protagonised encentre my role that
i may play the tune no solo whole though oh play it mid-
pitch c-major on an english horn so the soft brass can chase
the wind; not for fame teacher never for fame my taskmaster
fame is the burden of the lonely the distinguished never for
fame only and always for conformity fame is the burden of
the distinctive tune me i do so want to do well bring me to the
middle i want us all to be the main part teacher to be far from
the darkness at the edge of the herd where individuals are
picked off as prey but in the tune we look out for each other;
thank you for showing me teacher good teacher lovely teacher
distinguished teacher i hope i do well master good teacher

Underscore

To underscore is to lose.
And that's where lines must be drawn.

<u>SACKED</u> and <u>FIRED</u>
For poor performance
After three months
Of negligible impact.

To underscore is to lose
To underperform.

<u>DISPIRITED</u> and <u>FRUSTRATED</u>
Spectators bayed for blood;
Heads on a plate;
Eyes roll
'Only one goal in five games.'
Never mind the 4-4 draw the match before.

To underscore is to lose,
To be the failed investment.

In the ice-tiled dressing room
The cadaver caves.
Team long gone,
Head in hands

He wonders why the fans who sung of his arrival
So quickly turned on him;
Without the English vocabulary
To express his distress
To his underscoring team.

"In Italia, io ero grande"
He whispers to himself.

Broke

Money cascades out of my ears
And nose and I stream with pounding tears
Smashing from eye to cheek
Like an arcane arcade payout
Credit seeps from my butt crack
Excess cracks my brittle skin with lack of lack
And my back hunches bows
Breaks turns twists
Like a raptor but weighted
Anchored to a post by greed and fear greed and fear
Wings crumple and my spine
banks and spirals under the collapsing
foundations of the world that I once soared above
That is, before its poles swapped.

My lungs are full of paper writ and signed with promises,
Choking me.

Fear

I see a photo of them,
From before elopement jokes crumbled.
An oldesque chemical technicolor print,
            tinted purple, a rich iris purple.
Models for a cruise ship of course,
Sailing into a maroon oblivion.
They have tried to gloss out the little index on her eyebrow
Which forever marked the thrill of being now.

The instant fear,
Of a bolt
Shooting a sharp tunnel through her eye;
Of a teenage girl's impulsion;
Of speaking out with a steel stare,
Now it is done, and I am young.
That moment, when clasping her fluffy-cheeked boyfriend,
She feels lost and ageing in a changing
Unstoppable, non-negotiable milky current,
And wills herself to hang the consequences
Kill the question, 'what comes next?'

As they drift towards Nirvana on idyllic waves,
I am the sea, bearing them away from me,
Nudging them further, further so I will forget.
I hear her whisper:
I channel all my anxieties
Into one sharp pain.
That moment is pure fear. It's like injecting
Adrenalin exactly into your soul.

Drift on, my fear.

I drop her, flat as a brochure,
On a veneered table.
Together they lie, immediately casualised
By a half-mooned vulture,
Who sees with crows' feet
Only a corporate ideology,
A purple logo and a white embossed tagline.

O

Torn 360 degrees
The pain of a molecule split - no longer
O2, lone ozone, breathless,
O! I cry O O O
That disappearing rag.
Memories rag.
The hole widens.

Until I the numeral for 1 describe myself
As the O of a tale that opens 'Once ...'
O am empty
O am torn
O have become nothing
Because there is no you and O.

Service

Helmand, Afghanistan, freelance, shadowing
a surgeon at a makeshift hospital, never again

Grab me a latte!
Jack?! A latte!
Shove some cinammon in - it is Christmas after all.
Here come the troops!
1, 2, 3!
Hieronymo!

As the plane drones closer
I nick a gaze through the red haze;
Paper curtains separate the wards.
These men hurt more than films,
But feel less real.

Someone get that music off! Where's it coming from?

He is the commander here,
Wielding healing weapons,
Knives that save lives,
Gassing his own men, to keep them brain-dead
Soporific as the dust in the air.

'Snow is falling, all around me, children playing, ha--'

THANK YOU!

The 'chutes open white circles above
Hailing a brief clatter of shots.
Aliens, angelmen, santas
Float in on a hot wind
So he can repair these men
And get them back in service.

Where's my latte?

When did you last see your family?

Handshake

My glowing seven-year self was darkened
               believing his handshake
Separated us like sea depth from heavens, and was subtitled
'No closer boy.'

But as his hands shake like a heat haze,
And he unclips his breath-vapoured apparatus
To see me better, and clasp the dust and sweat
               of his boy's palms

I feel seven again ... and never closer.

Errant

J. Errant Flynn – known to the world as Errant
With a voice as deep as honey
And sweet as coalmines;
Melodies captured from the negro slave standards
Rehung, slung on the staves dripping,
Tripping rhythms and smooth like lemonade;
"Oh Mamma" (these words were for her),
"Oh Mamma, I'm gonna
Curl ya hair fa church tomorra."
Errant was smooth. Smooth like acorns.
I was a fan,
With signed vinyls that kept me going
Through the valleys and the shadows.
I owe a lot to Mamma.

Clandestine

Napoleon rears up on his horse, there is victory in his eyes

If you could look over your shoulder,
Turn your stiff neck to see,
See me hounding your steps,
Stalking.
Walking ten abreast with my brothers
Glinting clandestine as a Sabbath morning,
Manes ablaze, fangs shining,
Eyes like lightning, howling, barking,
Crouching, clawing, springing,
Tracing your every move;

If you could stretch your aged muscles to see
What darkness will not conceal,
Evaporating starlight spots reveal,
Then you would save yourself.

Our attack is secret only because
You are afraid to admit it
You will not crane or cower or smell the scent of your own
Glistening fear,
If you turned,
You would be dazed by your destiny.

Eversands

Paris left far behind, below, cooling like a spring;
Ecuador, an old thought, a child once aborted;
The new adventure my pen has drawn to me,
The glorious Gobi Eversands.

Up here, Errant fills my ears with a rescued refrain,
"All other ground is sinking sand"
And I soon drowse,
Feeling the warmth of the airs shimmering.

The endless nihilism of the place will dry my skin.
What is there to see? Why has my pen called
Me to a bleached region of tiny grains?
Millions of handfuls huddled on these plain plains.

Lights unlit
Allow me to unplug,
Alight from my seat.
I'll walk the aisles when my knees feel varicule.

Not a drop to drink; survival – endural
I will parch and I will flake in the Eversands.
But isn't that the bulls eye of a story?
"All other ground is sinking sand.
All other ground is sinking sand."

February Wreath

The evergreen halo, nailed through the door,
Turned brown as the nights grew longer;
Waxed spines waned, crisped, and some dropped,
Or, dug through the holey leaves surrounding it and remained,
        silent.

As epiphany passed, and bluebells crept through the
        frosty soil,
The brass knocker disappeared into the background,
The black door, layered with the old street's pollution,
        stayed fixed shut;
The February wreath
The only mark they knew the soul inside had gone.

powder

the charcoal of my body
in the jar of the hermit-cremator
where gathered dust gulps mortal failings' fumes
where withered dear ones die to wheezing words,
to memory, and fantasy.

the pumice sand, my body
and my soul - and my stories - contained;
unscattered me scooped neatly, to entomb
unfettered, so folk say, from coffins' cold,
all-discomposed, not earth-enclosed.

the thunder knew some body
and she journeyed a fiery-wanderer
storm-clouded, hot, called Djinn, smoke churned to tales;
Now powdered sparks ignite, like faery fumes,
Older than breath; stronger than death!

Introduction

After a press schmoozing event in Dubai

I have a name I do not use
My father called me my father's name
And that is no small introduction.
At home and all through school I shunned the first appellation
In favour of the simple 'Jack'
A slant on my mid-name, which had no connotations
Of his Emmie nominations.

My card, passed round in speculation,
Betrays no hints of our connection,
Not even an H. to marry Errant's J.
I so far grieved my father
That I can no longer use the phrase
He deigned to be my introduction.

I remain his son, but I am just,
Jack.

Burial

I see
A woman
Old in experience
Young in years
And she lies in a pool of mud.
Nourishing mud slops over her.
A living muddy burial.

A funeral for memories maybe
Or alopecial stress.
The muck clogging her ears suppresses
The secret whispering fears
"I am becoming old."

She will leave her spa day
Glowing that she relaxed no end;
Dead to her old self.

Behind veils, scowling at her reflection,
She will grimace and despair that she does not look how she feels.

Tipping

The crowd goes wild,
A smash, a splintering
"Wahey!"
All part of the night's must-carpeted entertainment.

Wind it back a moment before the clatter
To the face of the terror-stricken waiter,
Struggling for balance and watching the tipping,
The tipping.

Wind it back just another moment
And the tension is there as his promiscuous
Gaze is returned with a fleeting flick by a bright pink dress
And admired pride trips off
Before tip, "Wahey! That's coming out of your wages mate."

Blink

When I closed my eyes for a moment,
I walked the beach with you.
Your arms were folded for the cold.
Needing to occupy my hands,
I threw stones over the ocean,
Tried to hide my heart;
How it begged you to be there when I reached Quito.

When I opened my eyes, for a blink,
I imagined rainy London,
Dreamed up a paint-fumed flat,
A veneered floor and an empty box of cling film;
A life that would never be real.

So I closed my eyes and walked the shore with you again.

Siphon

We're trying to siphon the meaning
Out of the Universe.
Crack the code
Face Sphinx riddles
Mixed up; turn hugs to kisses,
Rings to crosses
Multiply the nothing
And discover the crypt.
That code of death
Unsolved; unsiphoned;
A full tank of fire and light
Darkness and night.
Dark oil spills and spits.
We try to store it.

The Sphinx looks at the
Man, soon to be blind,
Soon to fall from three legs
To lie as a slug in the ground
And be eaten by worms
And tube-rats.
And, problem solved,
She throws herself into the dark water.
Is she laughing or crying?

Pilgrims

On finding the Prayer Room at Damascus airport
empty save for a large pair of shoes

These are not my shoes.

It's an odd procedure
But the little girl refused to
Put it down.
It lies
Anaesthetised and hotly lit,
I prod metal toys through the mange

Conducting a procedure
Alien even to experienced fingers.
Playing God. Playing Surgeon. And ringed with a heady halo.

That's when I feel the pinch in my toes,

I find my mind joking in the voice of my father,

      "You walk a mile in my shoes,

        You get blisters Big Foot."

He puts his cup down.

"How can anyone believe humans are distinct from animals,
Mos? Look at the anatomy of a cat, Mos! Skeleton, muscles,
brain, there's really no difference."

      "Except animals don't pay zakat," I joked.

The nurse mops my forehead, looking demeaned.
I'd apologise but my hands are
somewhat splayed
inside a cat.

And these are not my shoes.

I sweat profoundly, sporting the shoes
of some Damascan Zealot,
While mine, God knows where they've got to;
Pilgrimaged to Mecca may be
or Mumbai.
After a moment's drowse
Cairo flight
1356 called, tumbling
sleepily, I
made the wrong
pair mine and left
some poor soul frowning
with bobbling, toe-holed socks.

Counting minutes,
I imagine my old shoes, pilgrims of the world.
They explore pavements, peer into cracks,
crush ants,
See the tops of bowed heads, hear the dirge cries of "Why?"
while God is a cat they won't let die.

Mashriq

Not long ago, that was me,
Clutching the sides of the open truck,
All smiles to the juddering phone video,
My headdress trying its darnedest to fit me
With the desert men's ways,
As we bounced along no-tracks
Kicking up dust and oil fumes.

They welcomed me with piled plates
Of pitta and mutabbal;
Perfumed us with tahini, pomegranate, fetté, green olives;
We laughed like jackals and they promised the coming
Good morrows.

I absorbed the Mashriq mornings
Where the waking souls rose,
Before the sun
At the mu'addin's call:
"Allahu akbar;
Hayya 'alal-falah."
The melody brayed from the tower
To the world around.

Some days, I knelt in quiet places where the old Levantines
Breathed their prime prayers,
Rehearsing Christ before Pilate;
Before I returned to be pressed like a washed shawl
In the haggle for dates.
"Mister, good price, good price, mister!"

They spoke about the future plenty,
But their prophecies
Detailed none of their desire for a declining West,
For Nineveh to rot, for the Damascene road to burn,
To play Pilate to thousands.

Now my head twists through spiny in-breaths of pomegranates,
The hot engine vapours, the rust, the fuel, the dust without end,
As I see them,
Men like my friends, men like me,
With guns that have killed others.

Too-hot feelings mix
And I switch off the news in fear.

Penny

In Mumbai, a penny is as worthless as a cork
As meaningless as a locket.
In Mumbai, a little boy took my copper circle
Eyeing it with, was it wonder or disdain?

"Sahib, may I keep this picture of your Queen?"

Near

Mumbai

"Do you live in the Near?" he asked me
And I have to say I wasn't as offended
As I might have been.
"Not the Near, no. Not now."
It was my low slung jeans,
And the feeling of sweaty Bronx confidence
I give off. An act, of course.
But one prevalent in 'The Near.'
Crossed paths have often caused me Near grief.
Bear-hands have scrapped to grab my shirt
And rip my wallet from me.
I'm fast though. I sprint
Out of the darker side streets of the Near, the bandits,
The Hell-hounds, the Sharvaras, the Near-terrors
Wheezing green coughs; I elude their claustrophobic
Klepto-manic clutches.
"I'm from Fair and Further," I reply
To the non-plussed, disbelieving old guru.
"Either way, pull your trousers up son," he says.

Daddy

Osaka

I'm surprised by the big eyes, yes,
But what gets me is the unreserved joy
Of the father. Pointing to his baby girl,
His smile, no eyes, all teeth and tongue.
He does not seem a small man
Cradling his family, he shouts
He sings, he dances.

Mesmerised, I'm surprised by the tiny fingers, yes,
But I'm undone by a tug of envy.
I've never before imagined being called, 'Daddy,'
Now, for the first time, I feel the thrill of that thought,
And the swell of pride.

If that were my name ...

I'm surprised, by the new life, the potential, yes,
But more, I'm in love with the idea.

Mist

Three days before moving home for good.
I found this poem scribbled on a napkin,
possibly linked to 'Tipping'?

Far off, the vapour forms a clear cloud.
Inside, the cloud clears
And standing in the mist of it all
We do not see the mystery,
That those looking in
Imagine.

Acoda

Spring wings acodas;
Winter is ending, birthing
A new overture.

Evelyn

Lake Garda

"Just visiting," she touches her ear lobe,
flashing sideways eyes.

He takes up his wine glass and crosses to
her table; slides himself onto a hopeful seat.
They flick at each other. Her eyes bolt first,
breathing shallow, and she looks out of the
restaurant across the little quay at Sirmione.

Gulls glide and turn, swooping for scraps.
The beaches here gather stones in small
heaps beneath the sheer walls of the quay.
Red-shouldered children stand by the
lapping water and laugh as they waste
pebbles perfect for skimming in splashes and
expanding ringlets. Others dunk their faces
into the lake, rising again with a gasp, their
eyes teary. They are trying to spot the little
minnows that swim in the shallows.

Yesterday brought a storm and now the air
has cleared.

"I grew up here," she ventures, looking out
over the lake. It's a surprise, because she has
never betrayed this before. This conversation
has been rehearsed a hundred times but, as
his gaze passes across her lips, he sees the
words are nevertheless unexpected. "My
family stayed here for seven years, then
we had to move on with Papa's job. We saw
... everywhere. By the time I was 12, I had
visited the Taj Mahal, the White House, lived

in Paris for a year and Quito twice. We were happy; my brothers looked out for me.

But my mother became stretched like worn elastic. She loved the adventure, but couldn't keep leaving her friends. She only wanted England.

My father argued that he couldn't provide the same lifestyle there. For a while, he forced us to travel, but during our second placement in Ecuador, mother became fatigued. When Grandma got ill, he gave in, and took us home. He was right, it was a shock not to be able to have the best things. And so cold. Sometimes I didn't believe our house had central heating. I hated it.

After three years, father came into a little money and brought us out here again for a week. Back to the heat, the fish, the freedom. That was when I felt for the first time ... something I couldn't have missed when I was younger, because I never had it ... Home. I missed home. Grandma and her witty stories. Corine, my best friend. Baxter chasing deer through Blenheim Park. I forgave my mother.

A year ago, a man I loved deeply offered me the world and I couldn't accept. He thought the world would make me happy. 'Life' to him meant keeping his freedom, escaping his ties – like my father. I was afraid of that kind of man. I let him go."

The waiter tops up the wine. He is about to speak, but, like the man across the table, who has been surprised by clandestine tears, he finds no words.

"I suppose a year passed. Then I saw our picture – leaning over a boat rail in a purple sunset - a silly, idealised advert on the back page of a magazine. It brought the whole thing back. I had already booked to come here again. I re-persuaded myself every day that you wouldn't be here waiting. Then I looked up and ..."

"I saw the picture too."

She stops. Holds her breath, silent for nearly a full minute. Then she's in tears too, covering her face with two smooth hands, unadorned except for freckles.

"I imagined you'd meet someone," I say, "And that would be that, you'd settle down with them, be one of those women who take mud baths in spas for holidays."

"Really?"

"May be not spas. What have you been doing?"

We talked until late into the night – I found out about the few false starts and romances she'd had, laughably tragic on the whole, and how, since the day she saw the brochure image again, she had occupied herself reading Calvino in Italian for the first time. She heard my side of things; about my parents. How I visit but never see them. That they are powder. But that something she'd said had made me turn for home before the end and for that I'm forever grateful.

Again, we refined 'us', astonished that feelings built on imagination and gaps were so strong in us.

Once we'd been asked to leave the restaurant so they could close, we walked the shores of Garda. Fresh in the half-moonlight and warm, we rediscovered each other, careful to say only what we meant. Several times, I tried to touch her, brushing my hand on her arm, but she withdrew from me. She was wary too not to fold her arms.

Collaborating with the chorus of nightjars and crickets, we gave the empty night both life and interest. It was a serious talk, but we laughed a lot too. When she found out that I'd lost my job and gone freelance as a failed statement of bravado, she giggled like she was a child again.

I understood in a new way the courage she had to turn down the romance of travelling the world with me, and that the night on the beach before I flew to Ecuador was her unsuccessful attempt to shoot through her fear just once and without regret.

"How could we have gone on loving each other for so long?"

"Loving?"

The world is full of such joy sometimes.

"I want to settle with you, Evelyn." We both know this is the right word. Like stormwater finally resting in a still pool so the sediment can drop, leaving the water clear. I want to settle.

She looks deep at me, and I hear Errant singing from her lips, "You never were a stranger, on any path I trod." And as dawn's diadem envelopes the mountains behind us, I know she has been waiting for Aurora to cast her silver train over the lake, to see me straight, to know me, to siphon her last doubts, to break her last fear. She allows her hand to slide into mine.

"I want to see the world with you, Harry John," she says.

I want to say we did more than laugh and cry, but that's what happened. The sun swept the shadows to one side as if they were dry leaves. The gulls woke up and gathered the thermals in their wings. As tiredness replaced conversation, we took to looking at the lake, and occasionally at each other. And then we would laugh and cry again.

Honeymoon

In the space of a day, a ring
And a party,
I move to 'us'
From a man
To a body
From solo to duet
From someone who knew
The word
Honeymoon
To passing you your dressing gown.

Glossary

All terms used in the context of these poems

Acoda	literally a-coda; against the coda. At the point where one thing is ending and something new begins
Blink	a fantasy or memory experienced with eyes closed, deemed to be a more real and desirable state than reality
Broke	state of having too much wealth
Burial	mudbath
Catch	a fish you should release for someone else
Clandestine	a shining secret that catches the light
Courage	making difficult, correct choices away from idealism, and even romance
Demi-second	a divinely lengthened split-second
Djinn	a genie, especially in Arabic or Oriental mythology
Errant	J. Errant Flynn; a fictional singer based on Ruth Naomi Floyd
Evelyn Walters	(aka 'E'), My wife
Eversands	a desert as experienced from within it
Faery	magick
Fear	channeling anxiety into a moment, or an object in order to defeat it with a single blow
February Wreath	a lonely winter ending in death

Flick	catching someone's eye and feeling something for them
Handshake	a gesture that, at first distancing, strengthens relationships through repetition
Hesperia	Italy in the evening
Honeymoon	a concept for the unmarried that can become a unique reality overnight
Index	mark that points to something else (in this context, a scar)
Introduction	a name, ie. how you would be introduced to people
Io ero grande	I used to be great (Italian)
Judgment	where an outsider interprets suffering as punishment, but the one experiencing the pain has a deeper (refined) understanding of the struggle
Lethian	named after the River Lethe, a river in the Underworld, which, if drunk from, brings forgetfulness
Mashriq	'the place of sunrise', in my case, Syria before the rise of IS
Mist	the quality that our lives have of looking plain to us from the inside, when onlookers believe them to be mysterious

Near	a ghetto modeled on New York Bronx culture, but not in the US
O	I without E
Penny	a coin of no significance outside England
Pilgrims	lost items
Powder	cremated ash, but still full of fire
Refined	re-defined in the context of a relationship between people or a group of people
Rehearsal	a journey on the London Underground
Rose	my laptop, on which I have typed this series
Service	refers to the mechanical aspect of being a soldier or a surgeon doing military work
Siphon	cryptic crossword clue; four across, six letters, 'Decant riddler mixed up with times becoming nothing'
Snow	a beautiful Zulu orphan aged about 12 when I met her; Snothanda means 'we love her'
Thanatos	Greek god of Death
Tipping	the moment when a waiter drops a tray and everything he was carrying will certainly smash, but hasn't yet
Tune	the norm / status quo
Underscore	failing, particularly in the context of a football team, but can be applied to ratings and response to travel-writing articles